Memories of Adulthood

Joel Rosenblum

iUniverse, Inc.
Bloomington

Memories of Adulthood

iUniverse books may be ordered through booksellers or by contacting:

iUniverse
1663 Liberty Drive
Bloomington, IN 47403
www.iuniverse.com
1-800-Authors (1-800-288-4677)

ISBN: 978-1-4759-1065-0 (sc)
ISBN: 978-1-4759-1066-7 (e)

Printed in the United States of America

iUniverse rev. date: 4/27/2012

DEDICATED TO THE FOLLOWING: my chef, my valet, my chauffeur, my physician, my arbiter, my critic, (all the same person: darling Joie)

MEMORIES OF ADULTHOOD

the ear's recollection speaks its ghosts
the mind sorts through all the voices

THROW DRAMA FROM THE TRAIN

I wish I were taller
I'd live to do Mahler

in all of his various oeuvres

a broiler, a brawler
a bull-and-cock scholar

shall we be shakers or only just moeuvres

EDGAR ALLEN POEtry

like words,
crouching
in their
dictionary...

awaiting release
through discovery;
become something
fictionary...

A DRAWING

the perfection of limb
every gesture of the pencil

reminds me of himb
though he's so reprehencil

OBITCHUARY

half hold
on a scaffold
but still in love and baffold.

CONTRA VERSEY

you and I have nothing to rehearse
the arguments, the quarrels
are *de rigueur* and worse

a marriage without morals
the click-clock of the verse
now attorneys do the orals

all talk forever terse

SKATING ON THICK ICE

drop me a note and let me know how you're doing
getting some praise or the usual booing

SAFE

Poems rise from sorrow
I guess I'll die tomorrow

I get to say
this every day

we are all lottery tickets
tossing in life's barrel
forever in turmoil's thickets
Death's angel pass over my camouflage apparel

NOT MUCH ADO ABOUT SOMETHING

Gods are made by fools like me
Let the gardener work on the tree

what's the point of cleaning all about
when you know you never throw anything out

scatter your beauty while others believe in
it

LAUGHTER IS BRAGGING TO OTHERS YOU'RE LOVED

there is one thing we all share with God:
Like the Almighty, we too love to take praise

TIJUANA, MEXICO

Italian chef Caesar Cardini
mixed such a distasteful martini

we needed this ballad
to praise Caesar salad

thank God that it's not Caesar's weenie

Heidi
had vareity
when her neity
revealed her entirety

EX EDGE ESIS

The whale
to his frail:
"You've quite a corpus,
and you did it on porpoise."

David Cassidy
So placid, he
turned acidy

THE QUALITY OF BEING HEAVY

bare earth, mostly when crawling
sky, ever so enthralling
depths only if falling
love me or are you just stalling?

HARLOT'S SPIRIT

a day *rigueur*
a kiss somewhere

EXPECTATION OF A MONTH OF MAY IN SIENA

room and board:
Rome and bored:
rum and beard:
Roman broad:

MERDE(R)

the cat does its doo-do
five times a day

not being a quitter
means plenty of litter
doesn't this critter
get tired in the sitter

A I R A T I C

Love is the well too many times I've been to
one drinks from this well but shouldn't fall
in to

LET'S FIGURE OUT WHAT THE HELL WE DID

courtesy occurs whenever you dance
memory is a bill paid by chance
love is the poetry of circumstance
sex is affection that goes without pants

THE INDECISION OF THE JUDGES IS FINAL

-the prayerful love God
the atheists hate H(h)is awful plot
the agnostic is seen
in between
doesn't know whether to take a holiday off
or not

God, the ultimate muse
lets you choose

among each and every letter
to write so much better

so how about a novel
cause close friends to grovel

or at least a Broadway show to
make everybody go to

maybe a sonnet
my genius get on it

tomorrow
I can borrow

can't a
Santa

amuse
a muse

get down, Jesus
finally please us

tired of rhyme ?
so I'm

HERE'RE A FEW REFLECTIONS FROM A KNOWN ADMIRROR

how to be nice is successfully self-taught;
how to be nasty must be guessed at and then
endlessly practiced

the muse advises but never approves

the best time is knowing that the best time
is coming

the brain not only has to think;
it has to battle the libido all day

You must create in order to evaluate yourself

Just because you never finish doesn't mean you
shouldn't be starting something

art is just education without menace

all musicians are black, especially the
Jewish ones

which is more endurable: boredom or
ridicule...?

self love
is a waste of time
it lacks the energy of hedonism

drinking just gives you a more pleasant way
to waste your life than life does

PURR DIEM

carpe diem:	seize the day
carp diem:	seize the fish
carpet diem:	squeeze the rug
car per diem:	public parking
carport diem:	private parking
carpool diem:	share the day
carpal diem:	bone *jour*
corporal diem:	army pay
corporate diem:	expense account
Cuerpo diem:	Tequila sunrise
clasp diem:	seize Doris Day

..SOME UNHEARD DIVINE WHISPER BECKONS US TO EXISTENCE

...everytime someone dies, God has failed..
everytime someone is born, mankind is saved.

the more good things life brings you
the more you decide you deserve them;
when the bad times come, it's God's failures

While you puzzle over this,
God is patiently waiting
for His next entertainment

To me, the world is full of innocent women,
and I am their lawyer

Don't fall in love.
I saved you only because I'm on.

Otherwise, the wind blew you gone,
my dove.

God says: "Just because I taught you a prayer
doesn't mean I understand your doubts.

BECAUSE YOU ASKED

a reason there is God is that to Whom would
we be trusting the bygone dead souls of
our departed loved ones if there were not a
Supreme Being waiting to do so

a reason there is God is to provide the
atheists with conversation

a reason there is God enables you to play Him
whenever someone sneezes

a reason there is God makes this one the best
sunset yet

a reason there is God has mostly to do with
the infernal permanence of art

a reason there is God while I'm at it is that
I am just as capitalized as He is

a reason there is God is that the word "GOD"
is actually also an acronym for Going On Dead

a reason there is God cannot slow down
overpopulation

a reason there is God can't slow down
overcopulation either

a reason there is God mystifies the firing
squad

a reason there is God exhausts the bigots

a reason there is God is the football fan's
last possibility

a reason there is God suddenly slows down
some of the farewells at the cemetery

a reason there is God inspires the artists to
make everything look better

a reason there is God enables us to explain
death to our children and life to our
grandchildren

a reason there is God can be summed up in
ten commandments:

                thou shall not
                thou will not
                thou can not
                thou must not
                thou dost not
               thou thinks not
                thou sees not
                thou tries not
               thou wastes not
               thou astro not
              thou sailor's not
              thou stoppest not

every poem is a lovesong to some unknown
person you want to possess

science fiction is right wing and sexist which
is why only men read it (women would love the
parts where everything goes wrong)

time lost in prologue first needs
a good drowning in any bar

it can't be wrong if I'm in love with
ssssssstreaksssssssssss
dots and spots and dabs and stabs no one
sssssssseeksssssssss
I've had this concept now for many
weekssssssssssssssssssss
the more the villain
sssssssssssssssneaksssssssssss
the more the mussssssssssssicshreiksssssssss
y
i
p
e
s
!
what's next?
s
t
r
i
p
e
s
?

somebody please put the apostrophe
wherever it's gotstobe

the cute as a species don't age well

rich men's illnesses change like any other
fashion

DELUSIONS OF ADEQUACY

WHY GOD

I don't know why God sometimes has blocked my
way but I do know why God has shown me the
way in the first place

I don't know why God is our excuse for forced
prayer in schools but I do know I made a
silent appeal before many a test

I don't know why God wants us to pray to Him
every day but I do know some things to utter
if I think I'm dying

I don't know why God provides His share in
holding off overpopulation but I do know that
war and famine are not His doing

I don't know why God gets His name on the
coins but I do know He's always endorsing
that blank check called Your Life

I don't know why God loves the little
children but I do know He refuses to keep
them out of restaurants

I don't know why God seems so serious but I do
know He laughs whenever I tell him my plans

I don't know why God takes an eon and sex
takes a second but I do know that's why woman
is called the second sex

I don't know why God decreed prayer and
fasting but I do know that the saddest
prayers are the ones asking for food

I don't know why God let Adam name all the
animals but I do know he should have called
the snake 'no-good sonuvabitch'

I don't know why God lets Christmas suddenly
end but I do know Santa Claus can visit those
you love anytime you say so

I don't know why God still wants to be
bothered with doing the weather but I do know
He raises hell with real estate values (and
shouldn't "Hell" be capitalized just to look
scary?)

I don't know why God allows computers to
replace people but I do know we'll always
have people because God knows you can't
punish computers

I don't know why God didn't make boredom a
sin but I do know this has gone on too long.

the poet writes for himself
the novelist writes for the publisher
the playwright, for an audience
the essayist, for the student
the humorist, for other wits
the psalmist, for God
the researcher, for academia
the genius, for posterity
the pamphleteer, for rebels
the copywriter, for suckers
the untalented, for fun

LEAR IN THE STORM MACBETH IN THE NIGHT

write! write! write!   thou bursting poet!
quick! quick! quick!   ere critics know it!

HOMOSECTIONALS

G a y c o u c h e s
(A n d n o o u c h e s)

Remember, the ear for imitation never gives
up its vigilance

life means taking care of others
death is taking care of others without being
appreciated

do blacks get tattoos/do reds get the blues\
can Olds still make the news

IMPOSSIBLE

climb the Himalayas on roller skates
swim the English channel in drunken states

stop the churchbells' Sunday ringing
radial tires no longer singing

sneeze and still keep both eyes open
lose your love and give up hopin'

car keys lost but no one hunts
blow and swallow all at once

play some tennis while the net is down
sneak the dawn past rooster clown

teach an elephant how to dance
ask your wife for a cash advance

matzo balls served in fresh clam chowder
squash small children when they're loud and
getting louder

fitting Cinderella in a size 10 shoe
giving up a really really bad tattoo

figure out the reason for the sand and all its
granuals
feel like a lion in a den of Danuals

try to comprehend what you cannot stop
like nature or chaos or people who shop

like family feuds, jury verdicts, a blood
transfusion
your wife from drawing the wrong conclusion
social tedium and empty train
the occasional failure of novocain

we can't figure out all the world's workaholics
but if they ever stop, then we'll all be
bucolics

make a strike in baseball count the same as
in bowling
it just won't rhyme but stop a wolf from
howling

BE WHICH ??

A sorceress makes a command which
excites every real dramaturger

she's pissed that she can't be a sandwitch
as she sits on the beach with her burger

YOU WHO

CHARLIE CHAPLIN WASN'T THE LITTLE TRAMP; YOU
ARE

WHO'S THE ONE HAS TO LICK THE STAMP; YOU ARE

WHAT'RE THE FIRST TWO LETTERS OF URUGUARY ?

ANYBODY LEFT WHO IS *DISTINGUE* ?

NOW WHO'S GETTING DAMP: YOU ARE

A BAD JOKE COMING

alcohol and jewelry ; things get rollin'
see the new use for the semi ; colon

(it is also little loss to me
if we call this a colostomy)

yes, let's hate the semicolon
like the useless head of the demi *Bolyn*

no sense at all of mellow drama
it's just a little above a comma

REJECTED

it's just a little above a coma
I'm writing this drunk in Barceloma

PLAYING GOLF WITH A GUN

"I shot a 67 today."

"Second to holes-in-one, professional golfers want white teeth."

"First it's 'fore', then it's play; at least in tennis, there's 'love'."

"Don't golf if you can't join a club, swing a club and bid a club."

"Is niblick really an iron or just someone playing with your ear?"

"Irons or woods? My mother does the one, my partner's in the other."

"Persistence in golf is important especially when you are explaining yourself to football fans in bars."

"The slowest game in the world involves driving something into a hole; the fastest game in the world is when it slips out."

"A sand wedge gets you out of the rough and tastes great with mayonnaise."

"When I am drinking, I think of golf."

"When I go golfing, I think of alcohol."

"When I play golf today, the ball goes right through the little windmill."

theater's like baseball
my dear little wits
it somehow depends entirely
on runs and on hits

everything a beachcomber finds is a sign of
trouble and failure

an appetite like a chain saw

I never got to show my father that I'm as good as I am.
Now I'm the father and my son despises me

TIE ME

booze loses time
drugs expand time
weeds measure time
lovers find time
poets rhyme time
divorces take time
lovers leave in time
explorers waste time
nobody is on time

art's job is to convince us history is
charming

UH-OH

the toilet flushes by itself whenever you are
on it

psychotic survivalists are forcing your wife
to write to you once a week

what can you call someone who writes for a
ghost-writer

for every action, there is an equal and
opposite reaction of face-slapping

if dogs would learn to drink alcohol, they could
never be taught the sit-up part of their tricks

ouija needs separated and you'll see "yes" in
French and in German

if the penalty for murder is death by firing squad, then
they'd immediately have to hire another firing squad

no no, it's a man riding a headless horse

I read your book now untie me

Raise your nose as a sign of being snooty.
You will find it prevents the eyes from seeing
others.
You will also bump into a mirror.

TUSHY DOCTOR

How proctical

an eight-sided probe

How octigal
and, nurse, where's that robe

the great classical composers
invent haunting themes
and then spend several hours
tantalizing you
that they might return to them

Either everyone is looking at you, or
you are looking at everyone else.
Take your choice!
Everyone's looking at you
and waiting.

AND THIS JUST IN

I'm retired and a cute case
all work is a wreck

Won't pick up a suitcase
and seldom a check

I'm old and a nutcase
no fury; all sound

an open-and-shut case
of screwing around

I'm shot and a court case
my lawyer's retreating

involving a tort case
not torte as in eating

I'm trashed and a slower case
of mistaken identity

what i need is the lower case
to remain a nonentity

You're always a game; I play you.

When I lose at it, I'm the game you've been playing.

The silence of the Muslims makes Allah weep

the muse entices but never approves;
she inspires and then departs
leaving her aura of criticism

meanwhile, the mind goes on creating; the
brain explaining

art is just education without menace

evil exists to make life interesting plus we must decide
how much of it we shall tolerate...there is no beginning or
limit to goodness

good music immediately soothes out the sound of bad
music

Who would teach more about life than an actress?

She invented the veil as aphrodisiac.

She shows her magnificent capacity to laugh sincerely.

Actresses must not just captivate but also convince
audiences.

Then their authority ends in flowers and approval.

Other women just don't seem to hear the applause.

The burial place of Moses is not revealed so that we do not make a shrine of our prophet's tomb. Moses' staff becomes a snake, reminder of Eden.

HUMOR, THE DEADLY APHRODISIAC

CREATURE TEACHER

you can teach a cat about where to shit but
that's all he's going to want to learn

you can teach an elephant that big ears have
little pitchers but with a line like that, all
they'll do is trumpet

you can teach a horse that the damn water is
good enough for you so what's the problem

you can teach a flea that life's all a circus
except in the market

you can teach an old dog new tricks if you
will just allow him one lousy orgasm on your
leg next time

you can teach a fly that you care more about
how long he gets to live than he does

you can teach a toad to keep on with his
croaking but they don't like you staring like
that at their throbbing throats

you can teach a baboon anything you want but
he still looks upon you as another ape

you can teach a steer a Gershwin song like
"Embraceabull Ewe" but if you'll just move to
Hawaii you'll have a frond for life

you can teach a hen to pretend she's saying,
"Cluck" but if you stand very close, you'll
realize how bad she smells

you can teach a moth that the myth is in the
math
even though they're supposed to be butterflies
that haven't had a bath

you can teach a parrot to say, *"I'm sorry"* but
he'll call you a *rottenbastardsquawksucker*
behind your back

you can teach a bear to stand up on his hind
legs but watch out if he calls you *"honey"*
you can teach an owl to understand daylight
but never to admit he's just a well-dressed
bat

We're rich! The dog had insurance!

LAWYER DREAMS

so many dying dictators
so many dyeing alligators

should we not make haste of the first
and shoes of the worst

DE LUXE

it's di lewks
not di lux

it's the nips
not the tux
10,000 ducks
all amucks

down in the mouth
flying south

*HOBOPHOBIA IS THE FEAR THAT ALL TRAMPS
ARE GAY*

GOD

God makes us love art. We make God wait.

God still loves everyone. We have to love the
very same bastards.

God provides an endless fourth-of-July-
fireworks variety of weather. We plan where to
retire.

God isn't having anywhere near as much fun as
we are.

THANK

you think quiet is the same as silence
you think mourning never has due
you think I'm seeing your life through my
tri-lens
you think anyone ever knows you

THERE IS A TITLE LOITERING IN MY MIND

one more idol, one less saint
soon God makes us all an aint

I suppose every old scholar has had the experience of reading something in a book which was significant to him but which he could never find again! Sure he is that he read it there but no one else ever read it nor can he find it again though he buy the book again and ransack every page

WHOLLYWOOD

who wouldn't play the piano if the keys were
in the shape of breasts

who wouldn't think ladies first, especially up
the ladder

who wouldn't legalize prostitution if money
could buy happiness

who wouldn't confuse Prince Charles' Latin
with Sir Charles Laughton

who wouldn't want to be a tackle on a girls'
football team

who wouldn't be thrilled to walk naked
through a blind convention

who wouldn't want his name in the snow with
someone else's handwriting

who wouldn't be able to be a good husband to
a sleeping wife

who wouldn't get closer to the woman buying
drinks

who wouldn't be cheap if God were buying
souls

"PLEASE WELCOME JACK THE RIPPER. SO, JACK, WHAT'S IT AUOOGH

THANK GOD FOR MUSIC

without
it women
couldn't
stand
at a
microphone
and
express
some feeling
for
men
and
not
have
to
pay
any
dues
for it

UNLIMITED MARIJUANA TO ALL CONVICTS:

they'll stay happy and calmed down all day

everything that occurs will be hilarious
to them

there will be absolutely no complaints
about the food

if homosexual acts result, no one will
remember

and also no one will want to remember

automatic calming will result from
hearing, "Man......

repeating rock music will replace the
cost of having wardens

regular TV will be canceled by audio-off
ESPN2 morning "beach" shows

the prison laundry area can be used for
an all-resident dormitory

prisoners who escape will be back in
twenty minutes

guards will give up weapons and carry
holstered candy bars

the cost of the marijuana will be paid
for by the incarcerated

the scourge of Alzheimer's will vanish
among prisoners

for there will be nothing to remember
anyway

a plenitude of men optimistic about the
sexual availability of women will never be
unleashed again upon a vulnerable society.

still unsolved would be trying to find
serious police.

PARENT HESIS

THE DOCTOR scowls
and everything's medical
should I ask for more towels
or just stay poetical

THE LAWYER smiles
and fees become legal
his bill will run miles
my purse, paraplegal

THE BANKER reads
you know he'll be saying
we only meet needs
of those who'll be paying

PER VERSE

How come men love to fake love; women hate
themselves doing it

men go right on talking without thinking,
only as women are willing to do the exact
opposite.

men plan sex as an actual possibility that a
woman will tolerate anything.

men know that women don't trust them, and
they still go on explaining.

men gamble every thing every time; women
have already lost the bet

men hear the sounds of fight crowds; women
shudder

men want to save a little time for
themselves; women have already spent it

men sleep off their troubles; women haunt
their own nights

men won't wait, except for sex; women want a
child, an ally

men try their best to avoid the blame; women
love control

men say, "I need..."; women have already
supplied everything

men often suppose they've done all they can
do; women remember their first husbands

men understand motels; women ask why they've
been hooked again

men love their departed mothers; women help
with the continuing burial

men are bruised, boozed or bluesed

women are floozed, cruised or abused

UP DOWN ELEVATOR

Living in hotels
is a horrible hobby
all the luxury
is in the lobby

Living in a trailer is a step down

Living in an organ is a stop down

Living in ecstacy is a strip down

Living in chains is a strap down

Living in demotion is a stripe down

Living is stables is a stirrup down

up down

up down

up down elevator

ODE TO MYSELF

the reason you love art
is that no one interrupts you

the reason you love good food
is that your wife has a paycheck

the reason you love Clinton
is that liberals charm women

the reason you love movies
is that you can sit in an empty theater at
2PM

the reason you love travel
is that your wife gets drunk with you at the
airport

the reason you love homosexuals
is that they laugh at your jokes

the reason you love Fitzgerald and Wilde
is that you don't understand Becket and
Arabal

the reason you love fireworks
is that you can stare at the chicks all you
want

the reason you love aerobics
is that somewhere near the steam-room women
are showering

the reason you love dry sherry
is that your wife thinks it's better for you
than rye whiskey

the reason you love The Weather Channel
is that you need to have the exact same
information repeated to you every seven
minutes

the reason you love The Ten Commandments
is that They remind us of the failure of
religion

the reason you love West Virginia
is that you love states with two names - like
horny drunk

the reason you love seeing football huddles
is that you can imagine the rotten life of
the homosexual watching them too

the reason you love God
is that He didn't accept something dumb like
Beelzebub did

the reason you love politics
is that now it's interesting because it's evil
vs evil

the reason you love jazz
is that everybody's horny

the reason you love Duke
is that Sophisticated Lady and Caravan gave
jazz some major spin

the reason you love boxing
is that it's a thrill to knock some bastard
out

the reason you love Rod Steiger

is that in the taxi he still cared about that
candyass Marlon

the reason you love Canadian Theater
is that you know you'll get out of their
country before their winter

the reason you like old highschool friends
is that you'd love to take another shot at
her considering that the reunion's in the
convention room of the same motel

the reason you love coffee
is that at least that's something from
Columbia

the reason you love synagogues
is that God will provide parking

the reason you love sailing
is that all decent boats have someone serving
cocktails

the reason you love diet Coke
is that rum always wants a disguise

the reason you love fresh air in your room at
night
is that the automobile horns will drown out
the police sirens

the reason you love our guest today
is that it's Jesus Christ and the show's
coming to you live from Salt Lake City

EYE YI

when I say it aint broke so don't fix it
that applies to everything there is

when I run out of friends
the alcohol's no good

when I say, "One, Two, Three, Hup!"
I'm just counting on the other players to do
something

when I travel for more then three weeks
no one is there when I get back

when I forgot where my car was one night
I read all the writing on my credit cards and
there was still no way to find it

when I kissed you
it was in your eye and we were 14

when I lose my way
I can sometimes still find the men's room
light-switch

when I find out that time is of the essence
I hope they mean time served

when I want to smell good
I flash at least a hundred

when I try to pretend I'm sober
my bartender lets someone order for me

when I was seventeen
prostitution would always be joined to comedy

when I couldn't hit a grand slam
you were always just a touch down

when I gave up 30 pounds to wrestle you
the referee stopped the fight and left town

when I asked my accountant for money
he admitted he had failed me (his phone
rings)

when I find Jesus
will everything be fine or just me

when I vote for somebody
a Republican loses ground

when I tried to get respect as an actor
all the air suddenly ran out of the inflatable
doll

when I am naked, crazed and starving
everyone else is figuring out how to watch the
eclipse

when I attend synagogue, churche and mosque
God tries to explain Rush Limbosque

when I write poetry like that
someone draws a chalk-line around it

when I would actually meet someone's husband
it was tough to tell the usual jokes

when I finally got home
my wife wasn't there yet

when I figure out the difference between good
luck and God
already I didn't put God first

when I find my wife intruding on my life too
much
I go to her parole officer about it

when I fall in love
a woman is mistaken again

when I married with an eye to paradise
the other eye saw the ravages of abstinence

when I began to love classical music
jazz wrinkled all my fancy clothes

when I played their piano at a Havana
whorehouse
the barmaid said it was too loud

when I tried a sticky spray on my athlete's
foot
the other one gleamed and actually moved its
toes

when I saw your attorney smile
I finally was able to stop loving you

**WE CANNOT SURVIVE
UNLESS WE KNOW WHAT IS ASKED OF US.**

                    in your midst
                    is a poet
                    halfway blitzed
                    as always, so what

Literature tells while other art primps.

Sex can overrule all rivals though not often
enough.

Rituals are what pass the time while God is
deciding.

AD FOR EARLY STOCK MARKET QUOTES:
get a jump on the business day

(or try it later that night then)

CULTURAL VANITY

start off saying truth's a forgery
end up forgetting be fore a jury

MUSIC WITHOUT SOUND

o butterfly
why not a fly
infinitely poetic
insect so pathetic

anyone stops in his track
to see this creature
flaunting its back
that artistic feature

casually flits
midst life's airiest bits
how fragile 'tis
its agile biz

how vulnerable; no sloth;
no defense from moth
the persiflage
the camouflage

HUMMUS SEXUAL

quit a fairy?
adversary?

literary:
add verse airy.

       the night nurse checks the patient's
breathing
       and all lust can do is to lie there
seething

THE PROMISE OF MOUNTAINS

Birds clasp their treetops content to be
perchers
Not knowing there's as many faiths are there
are searchers

One dark afternoon I dug quite a hole
planning to vanish

But instead of the shouts of some Chinese
soul
all the sounds were in Spanish

MASSIVE DOSES

I've tried to get the meaning of trope.
No hope.

at least British royalty snubbed Eva Peron

THE WHOLE WORLD ARE hOLOCAUST SURVIVORS

how is the mind able to remember so much music?

the cleansing of the soul is commanded by the rushing sound of violins chasing their imaginary birds.

Laughter is God. If you are roaring with amusement, captivated by it for whatever seconds, you have God Himself showing you how to live longer.

Love always needs support from money; otherwise, it becomes torment or vengeance or uselessness.

-God wants us to understand islam
or is it god doesn't want us to understand Islam???

MOST SNAKES SAID:

don't pay any attention to the first humans; the Garden of Eden has plenty of other failures

hearing Rite of Spring inspires me to write a movie;
Shostakovich tells me I've already had that orgasm

The Chinese food 'dim sum' means dot the heart
(and fill it with cholesterol)

kiss me and then we'll kiss

There's just me and God; and without Judaism,
there's just me confused

But we are all learning how to combine hedonism
with waiting

BRAVOS TO THE YUGOSLAVOS

We should be forced to obey all poets
and treat them as if they're Pygmalion

We'd sing to the Serbs and the Croats
that this is what they get for not being
Italian

You must create in order to evaluate yourself

The fatal thing on figuring out computer
software is there are too many choices

-the heavy drinker just blows apart! You know
he's inside several coffins..

alcohol makes an explanation become a
description

Never write the poem's title first;
then you're stuck with a bad-ass idea

inhale her breath
now you know her
or, well, at least she's starting to believe
it

all the lives, places and times
freeze their knowledge
waiting out disappointment

and still designing love

Man's life is the experience of a chance to
know a woman, not just the inner fireworks

BOXING MATCHES

I gave up on boxing, you know. I simply got
tired of running around in drab, little
costumes and picking fights with perfect
strangers.

as if God hasn't taken care of me whether I
believed in Him or not

whispered between the two lovers
please stay beautiful; please stay blind.

MAMMOCKING THE BUTTERFLY

Terpsichore
visual trickery

how long will you wait
for me to figure out where we are
and not force a debate
(and not only in the car)

writing poetry is an extreme form of self-
praise

next you must either lie to yourself

that you know how to write poetry

Or else just stick to rhymes.

the word ""farce" has its root in the French
for to stuff as in chicken farci

SIGNS OF LIFE

no hitting on the break
no hitting on the bell
no hitting when down

no spitting in the lake
no spitting to help polish
no spitting off Pikes Peak

no knitting up the brow
no knitting up the ravell'd sleeve of care
no knitting unless sitting

no sitting unless knitting
no sitting during curtain calls
no sitting under the apple tree

no quitting till the finish
no quitting till closing
no quitting till the acquitting

no shitting in the cash register
no shitting on teachers
no shitting yourself

will whiskey bring luck ?
where is it I'm supposed to go ?

I T

what day is it? today
what time is it? now
what second is it? November
what year is it? our Lord's
what season is it? thyme
what way is it? my
what fight is it? grudge
what food is it? soul
what use is it? what?
what use is it? what?
what day is it? tomorrow

all Joel
is divided
into three parts

Calves,
liver,
and anchovy hearts

NOW THEN. GAYS!

why do they need defending

who's attacking them

they are loved by

musicians,
artists,
fellow gays,
their mothers,
Hollywood,
civil rights activists,
Jews,
clothing designers,
rich women,
jealous men,
sultans,
steam bath Staffs,
desperate sitcoms,
Hollywood Squares,
movies with 'airport' in the title,
hair-styling salons,
men's body magazines,
me.

WHIRLED TRAVEL

The rich know the good food;
The wealthy know the art;

The middle class, the tours;
The lower middles, the brochures.

I can't help rhyming
Even when I'm wasting timing.

Oh, and the poor know the free museums.
Same as the rich

   Islam a religion that preaches love but not
fairness.

AUTHOR OF HIMSELF

prose
a pose

to kill
the poetic
and still
stay prosthetic

Puertorican Priests: Latinos actually
speaking Latin.

   art is escaping into an instinct

HIGH THEY'RE

flu shot
blood clot
why not
smoke +'#*&^t
thnks alot

The Beedough twins, Lola and Nola
The Hoo brothers, Utch and Bora

VOYAGER

I can see another sailing craft
the white fragment of some distant vitality

visually imposed upon a mountain island,
now become one of its landscaped dreams.

scraps and tatters of cloud
rim the inverted heaven bowl of sky

now for plying that limitless ocean fluid,
raging for purity.

ineluctably saline

the sea's color,
jade of East, pulled from an idol's eye
a tongue, the lick of delight,
beguiles every wave as it lashes

the suggestion of a moon
now that it can again merely be dreamed at
begs its earth lovers to believe

ocean spirits freed from the tyrannous land
urge the mind to become their gentle master

and all conspire in this "mincing poetry"

P O E T R Y I S T H E S O U L
W R I T H I N G I N C R I T I C I S M

I care only for heroes and villains;
why are the rest of you crowding in the
middle with me

homosexuals merely reveal the hurt in life
that we other men are not allowed to express

LIKE A FEVER

love comes and goes without the will having
any part of the process

TIME

what you see is the real time
not the amount of minutes a watch is off
not daylight savings
not you're in Europe somewhere
not Greenwich being mean again
not time served
not time unde served
not the time while beauty explains itself
not the time remembering movie stars
not the time spent letting alcohol do the
lying for us
not the time fitness and money waste arguing
with love and fun
not the years trading off a dead woman for an
expensive one
not the hours played for time
not the moments when it seems the mind owns
the air, not the lungs
not the truces between the lies
not the days of wine and poses
not the expectation of midnight when it's
zero o'clock

poetry has only two inspirations
sadness or fun

FLORADA

Oranges - grapefruit
gifts all en route

but realize you're sending
fruit to a fruit

PRAYER IS REVERENCE; NOT MERELY
PETITION

   Though no one's understanding me
God keeps on overglanding me

YOU'LL RECALL

We planned on love

our choice was domination or surrender

a quarrel or a bender

or all of the above

PIANOFORTE/POETRETORT

I have the fingers and the time
let the keyboards do the rhyme

LAUGHTER

out loud and alone..
out of control now
with the realization
of recently having acted crazy

PREJUDISH

it must be hard being
black and gay
and what if you're also Canadian
eh?

SO OUR FIRST FIGHT IS IN THE BOOKS

can you find comedy
without comity
drinking like a dromedary
passing out the commentary

BROKE COCOA

baroque always gets drearier
with the usual inferior
rococo interior

WHAT? END THE MADNESS?

Just head your self sackwards
I'm floating in backwards

It's a matinee mood
meaning sex and junk food

Oh the wonder of any other
who's not one's mother

WHY SHOULD I BE UPSET

No one understands my play
any way.
Anyway,
I read it over every day.

Science goes on testing
the mysteries Everesting

A WAITING-ROOM OF KISSES

LOVE DOESN'T GET TO RHYME

they were in terror
having to prove
the error
of love
on the move

get it?!
"love" rhyme with "move"?
"shove" rhyme with "grove" (groove?)
forget it !

ARE YOU GAY AGAIN

some big and hairy
dignitary
catch your shadow;
you been had; oh
thank you very

witticism:

music, poems and and other abuses
are life's oldest excuses

for ignoring criticism

the absolute easy way to end anti-Semitism is
for everyone to become jewish. and no capital
letters either.

THEY'RE COMING! THEY'RE COMING!

God, we're all British,
brutish and skittish
broodish and skiddish
abroadish and quidish

money, the whore that promises change
and taunts you to prove you're secure

MERRY : WANNA

I pulled the few grains
from out of my pocket,
swore I'd never smoke lint after this
and then fired up my new treasure

reading is the act of avoiding arithmetic

NULLIFIDIAN PRAYER

God is not dead.
God is, instead
(the theory's so deep):
He is asleep.

PRE DICTION

that sunuvabitch Nostradamus
is shown to have broken his promise:

the whole world would end!
what we get is portend

all this time!?
let's just sail the Bahamas

millions more poets have viewed more goddam
paintings than the graphic artists have
bothered to read our shit.

as soon as you cannot keep anything from a
woman, you love her

HAM LETDOWN

Front to Sweden
Back to eden

NEITHER IG NOR ME

my pleas and my patheticals
charmingest poeticals

covert parentheticals
hate the antitheticals

HERE'S WHAT I WANT TO DO

end waiting
find benefactors
ignore facts
judge you
giveupthespacebar
marry a dentist
find some applause
end all experiments in rejection
stop imitating those whom I don't understand
locate the outskirts

ALI won the heavyweight title 3 times

GOD ACTUALLY SPEAKING

I'll restore Eden as soon as I get this
answer: if Christians love and revere the Old
Testament then why do they not support the
keepers. Point 2, their interest in the Old
Testament makes them Jews by evolution We
need to influence the goings on in Israel...
they are losing Judaism and, at this rate,
what's the point of a homeland for the
Abrahamics???

SCORE CARD

a loss is not death
take a deep breath

and Check the venue
God didn't take you

WRITE YOU ARE

baffled by poetry
left for dead

way out in limbo
existential dread

ring a bell
or someone's neck

who the hell
's a nervous wreck

THE ANCIENT marRHYMER

money instantly ignites love's flame

the sounds of infinity replace the silence

soon the mind plans to remember her name

and the whereabouts of the poetic license

SIR LUNCHALOT

You get to be the son I never wanted. Perhaps
we can click now that you're older than I am.
At least, conversation can involve something
other than the latest computer jokes.

RYE SLING

r i s i n g

sizing hippo
hip notizing

INTERCOURSE

We're on the cutting edge
attracting revenge

trimming hedge
failed coitus avenge

WHEN'S DAY

When people have no stability
they kill each other

when they want money
they overcharge each other

when they find mystery
they fall in love with each other

when life is impossible
they hate each other

when change is inevitable
they abuse each other

when people sing
they immobilize each other

when people say prayers
they confess to each other

when time begs for more people
they haggle about nooses

when love miraculously becomes life's giant
eraser

they discover they can get themselves back
again

As each city develops its music and theater
art and talent, civilization gains another
generation of sanity. Other artists create
pictures, images. We theater artists create
people. Actual living, feeling people.

....so it was just the need to cry;
not the need to cry <u>over</u> anything/something..

up in smoke
life's one long toke

hold your breath
life's one long death

laugh a lot
life's one long shot

CAPITAL BETTERS

it's really God and I
livin' out Our lives together;
so will He die
when I do, or dare I say 'whether' ?

there's an orgasmic merger:

the soul's thoughts
with the mind's braggadocio

WHY SHOULD I BE UPSET

WADING THROUGH SCHONBERG :

burning violins over-stoked with madness
having their pity sawed in two

I like the haunted silence of architecture,
which is the art dedicated individually to
each uniquely stricken wonderer

Unrealizing, whatever we paint, we are only
depicting pictures of God.
Odd that He responds by creating a 100%
different human being every time.

Love is actually everything there is in the
world excluding sin; which is the one thing
that is more fun than love.

Tipping recites someone's moments
spent under a tray

The one thing we always do when we are
indicating our sincerest dedication is to
close our eyes.

God first made me Jewish and then yelled at me
whenever I was stupid.

DR+NK

liquor straight
men not so;
sick or late
when got so?

*OVER 70(I'M TALKING ABOUT THE SPEED
LIMIT, DAMN IT)*

desire's ambition requires an electrician

   redundant tautological pleonastic periphrastic

   all these self-proclaimed august US Senators
and not one of them can come up with an idea to
save the other 99.

   *SEX CAN STOP LOVE FOR AT LEAST A
LITTLE WHILE*

ENTAIL

a flower's exhalation
charms the air

a story wept
is beauty's prayer

I KNOW ART BUT I DON'T KNOW WHAT I LIKE

poets like painters
pour their intentions
upon ladders of love
forgiving the moon
before time starts lying

you can't just suddenly not own a radio
station
it all stays in your head
still playing out the music
saying the words that sell

supplying sound, a choice
of music and voice

table d'hote always looks like something with
a few of its letters shot out.

GENE TUNNEY NEVER FOUGHT A BLACK FIGHTER

the poet's storm and drag
take form and do the rag

practice your English
the tongue hates rest

better to be singlish
than with marriage you detest

two things: this isn't funny
and who cares about Gene Tunney

DEAF INITIONS :

love, the excuse for continuing dreaming
and the only defense of the abused

Sex, the soul loves itself
and proves you can stop

Arrogance, the elegant response to
ingratitude

Software a girl should be soft

Music, the miracle of the perfect blending of
human souls

SADNESS IS NO SUBSTITUTE FOR OUTRAGE

BETRAYAL PORTRAYAL

paintings make their demands
they explain beauty
to the slumbering eye
demand instant opinion
from the colorless memory

THE EYES MIND

the eyes do the same thing
whether producing tears for the megamillion
dead
or providing the tears for finding yourself
safe
or the watered cheeks of love released
moisture unmastered
lost in loss
joy of escape

THE MINDS SIGH

then you want me?

I can make you either laugh or cry
both are easy

but you do everything else:
decisions, distress, tipping waiters

I ac knowledge
I lack knowledge

My life, pages in the wind

Call love adultery!
What insultery!

Love sets traps
and never gives maps.
What saps

these mortals be.

EXPLANATION THOUGH IT'S NOT NECESSARY

The sun doesn't move, the earth does
the dreams all improve when mirth does

If Eden is just the right step away
Then Jun, Jul, Aug and Sep away.

You can't take land from the owner's pen
'less the world's gone mad and hates Jews
again.

I asked for a God who should be as much like
me as possible.

YOU RARELY READ WHAT YOU SHOULD AND
YET

YOU'RE READING THIS

EXTRA VAGRANT

                    you can outwear
                     a love affair

                          the flow of hope
                           is exit's rope

THAT YOU

never take precautions
is too lost amongst the Martians

One writes or paints easily if only for oneself.

Art like love can be so wonderfully selfish!

when a man talks to God in the shower
the Almighty will know someone's praying
he's waited to bathe for an hour;
now pleads that the hot water 's staying

DOMESTICATING THE DARK

this is as poor a poem as I have written
by now you know that I'm not sh*****

*********'s are sissy keyboard nerds
all those **'s instead of words

aster****'s
are ruptured d****'s

***************'s are bosses
unless you dig +++++++++++++'s

for best things italia
siena corral ya'

lip a crit : he who talks while kissing

THE ANGEL OF SILENCE

lost time gets even worse
after good times disappear

nature's coinage reimburse
with every falling tear

HOSPITAL RHEUM

doctor: Well, how's my star patient today.

God: Dead.

doctor: Not you. I meant the sufferer.

God: Then give me a damn capital Y.

doctor: No, it was actually You. You, God, are
dead.

God: Just what We need. Another amateur
undertaker.

doctor: I am God.

God: No deal. I'm not going to be a damn doctor.

doctor: See? He still gets to do more Goddamning than I do.

God : The reason you can't be Me is you see Eternity and a doctor's charges as the same thing.

doc: Why doesn't doC spell God backwards? Also, Mr. Eternal, I prevent far more deaths than You do.

God: 214,622,484 people died last year.

doc: So?

God: So where were you?

doc: I can relieve all pain to anyone I touch. You never do that!

God: Yes, I do. I call it death.

doc: Murderer

God: All right, doctor. I'll work out a resuscitation for your patient here in the hospital. He can live for 714 days more. Oh, and I have this great idea for you. An HMO for athiests! Whaddya think? Who could run it???

doc: Ohhhchrisssssst.......!

God: Brilliant!

Rainfall always provides three wonderful
options: the exquisite sound of a storm-
shower or all its many mysteries or just cozy
safety from it.

I was first astounded at all the cyberpeople I
acquired on my rolls
who read all my scrolls

nothing that one would repeat
yet somehow survive the delete

I ' m t o r n b e t w e e n t h a t a l l t
h i s i s j u s t h a p p e n i n g f o r m e

O r i t ' s g o i n g o n a l l t h e t i m e,
w i t h o r w i t h o u t m e

VAMP PYRE

if I can't be sarcastic
it's hard to write satire

I sound all bombastic
my prose like a flatire

never been a word for what you are if both
drunk and stoned WAIT! I got it! *Arrested.*

the race with God always ends in a tie

to decry the neurotic is to share with him

charity is momentary guilt
marriage is permanent guilt
Old people read everything now that they
don't have to do anything about it.muses may
die if they really feel they have to
writers find reasons for love
ecstasy is money, safety and air
conditioning
marriage is an attorney with a key to
your cell
drinking is that daily dullness of a
world already going
driving is when police are really apt to
notice you
money makes itself go round. can you do
that?
dancers charm by being weightless
while birds stand on telephone wires
architects define dreams
dancers can only be mirrors of music
religion challenges the vices
but has too few saints
islamism ismt
love remains the only explanation for
life
laughing at everything clears the room
of people not drunk
adventure proposed at the hands of others
best involves a hearty fare-thee-well
Men are all gay in that they love
sometimes
to be alone.
art, the crossword puzzle of the damned
jazz is what your mind writes
after you hear the first note
anger is a short madness

We waste so much time peeing. And we waste the same amount of time drinking. How the body demands its nonsensual attentions!

MASK OF TRANQUILITY ~ like an actress returning wearily to her room after a tiring third act and falling half dead upon a couch while the audience retains an image of her to which she bears not the slightest resemblance

something neither natural nor necessary
like giving up your seat to a woman under 14

                        courage imperils life
                        fear protects it

few people escape painting nowadays

the arts are selfish;
they create entirely too much mystery;
then they invade your self-confidence

watch out for cunning as in those
who profess unworldliness

PLEASE TALK IN SMALLER PRINT

winter is the spring asleep, all its flowers resting
soak up snowflakes' gentle waters, coolly ingesting

at least my modern proposals shall be cheery
like English bishops on the quantum theory

when, feeling the great boots of the rich on our faces,
we live in the hope of one day changing places

it is we not nature who abhor the vacuum
(you do mean the sweeper, don't you)

The sun that I see is but an image of an event that occurred 8 and one third minutes ago for that is what it takes for light to travel the 93 million miles that separate sun from earth

schizophrenia is life without metaphors

dedicated now to dear friend Marcus
who treats my lines like some old carcass

poems as useful as Latin trivia
I should have mailed them by way of Bolivia

or maybe just outside Carrarcas

POET TO HIS UNFINISHED MASTERPIECE

poet: I've been cheating on you. I've been
writing sonnets elsewhere.

MASSTRPEESE: I don't care, God. I like being
funny-looking.

Marriage is just spending a few years without
an attorney

WHAT'RE COLORS

There's nothing more disobedient than the
paintbrush

There's no activity that *dry sherry* does not
improve

If only *alcohol* could be turned into *colors*,
then we could drink and paint out of the same
cup

Books by artists do not tell you how to
paint; they tell you how they paint

Art depicts the past; science hurries the
future

        I don't know if I've ever been here before
                but I'm not here now

STO X NED

there are too many people who want drugs;
it's clearer
I liked it better when there were only three
of us:

me, you, and your mirror
when do you think you'll be free of us

RHYME RISKY

I'm not comfortable actually writing the word
f**k
I have indicated this by typing it out in
lower case
When I'm speaking, though, I am not so
awestruck
(there are many expressions I do not erase)
I have cursed out loud like a porn Donald
Duck
but I'm just nervous doing it in cyberspace

And another thing about THAT word in the dark
I am not validating it with a quotation mark

H A T R E D O F I R A N I A N P A V E D R O A
D S :
j e w I s h a n t I - c e m e n t I s m

Why are we addicted to storing things

all cyberspace does is send us someone else's
files

There is a glorious piece of early luck in a
long kiss

when the woman's mouth slowly recognizes it's
you

who sez not losing your temper makes you a
philosopher at once

I am not my brothers keeper; I'm his needy
sibling

magic exists as a response to anxiety

THE END OF ALCOHOL OR HOL

booze helps you hang on till Eve finally comes
back
to apologize about being hungry that one day

this is Eve,
God's realization that man needed a companion
in life

Eve also thought the snake was just some
talking, costume bracelet

The one portrait of Adam we always know is
the Sistine one where he extends his limp
hand to the entire furies and powers and
Armageddons of God

But Eve. Two sons and one kills the other
(the world's first holocaust)

And she knew about <u>apple</u> brandy right away
and also terrible daiquiris

She. Let us at this moment, praise our
moms and our wives. Since they manage to

find things to do while we are not around
bullshitting them

And She begets two sons; not a son and a
daughter or, God forbid, a daughter and a
son.

So you have God as the only Presence in a
mystical, unknown spirituality. He starts up
the cosmos and then experiments on a pebble.

And Eve could think, "Where's God been?
Where's He going every night? I have a naked
man, a bunch of fruit trees, a talking snake,
no comfort facilities, and He wants me to go
on a diet.

Eve though.
The soft respite of the tedious day.
The promise that requires nothing else.
A miracle, a non-man. An extra letter <s>he.
The only ego-builder that usually doesn't
involve immediate cash.

Her ageless temples are always open for
prayer and sexual fasting.

Eve gave humankind its most sacred word:
Mother.

THE TEN NOT EXACTLY COMMANDMENTS BUT NICE TRIES

try to stay awake if the bar's closed
try to remember if you can turn right on red
try to celebrate when you don't have your
credit cards
try to dance when only your feet are on the
floor
try to sound brilliant even if the music's
too loud
try to keep just the kiss going after you've
put your glass down
try to explain again how you know where your
car is
try to describe your play to people still
drinking only coffee
try to start a conversation with your
girlfriend's Afro-American father
try to accept that drugs are entirely too
expensive and you're still going to buy them

I FORGAVE YOU FOR MY SAKE; NOT YOURS.

classical music was at first very menacing as all those unprovoked emotions were being thrown at the young listener

Ah! the magnificent unfinished symphony by Franz Schubert although every composer's symphony is unfinished till somewhere it's heard

the best thing in life is yours forever,
even defying death; it's:

    N O W

if you kill the bird, the next messenger will
not have wings

the graciousness (discoverablity) of a leaf

Music gives God a lot of rest
Also, realize that He provides you with your
talents so He has someone to pray to for what
He wants.

TO RON TO RON TO

Go oat, if you're Canadian
Go out, if you will use as directed

Fifes and drums all paradian
Fives and tens soon rejected

CAN YOU HELP ME WITH DIALOGUE NOW?

ME: I like space;

YOU:

ME: Very good.

there are so many TV police programs the
viewers ought to have their rights recited
like everybody else

THE NUN OF THE ABOVE

God's good laws I've often kept
and for man's sins have duly wept
and when inside temple I've sometimes stept
have reverently crossed my hands and slept

the death of Satan is a tragedy for the
imagination

'TIS PITY SHE'S NOT A WHORE

ladies cage, then vacuum men
of their coins until obscurity

..if you want a rhyme again,
give up all hope of purity

GOD NEEDS MORE POEMS

the best way to help the working poor is to
let them keep their earnings.

grammar protects us from being at the mercy
of the tone of voice

I early learned somehow that Liszt was the
toughest composer for piano to perform. Added
delight is trying to make certain whether
it's one pianist or two playing the piece.

the reason you love to do poetry
is that God won't help you write a novel

the internet has changed our brains
we write people we don't know

THE VICAR OF WAKEFIELD

all our adventures were by the fire-side,
rare was a visit to mailbox or town

living was such we lived only on our side
and all our migrations from blue bed to brown

a curtsey, a smile, a family
a breeze that wafts both health and harmony

COGS AND DATS

GET MEOW TAVIT

BOW WOW TOF IT

YOU

you wouldn't know a sailor from a saint
just cause (not 'cause) they aint

neither one desires to live at sea awaiting
slaughter
both existing on little else but water

the trouble with alcoholics is that they
never call you when you're drunk, too

freedom enables the liberal to be right
and the underprivileged an opportunity to
struggle

"Maybe it's just that God's avoiding you" is
so funny I gotta steal it

to decry the neurotic is to share with him

IN ALPHABETICAL DISORDER

Well, authors are all echoes
dancers are all raised

artists El Grecos
critics too praised

Bartok 2nd concerto...zen is nothing more than
endless sabbath without worship.

SERENE wRAP

Snowfall, snowfall, have you any cheer?
Who the heck said that spring was here?

Let's not worry about global warming
Now that March has brought this storming.
We were all set for a nice, spring break
But don't look up 'cause it's flake after flake.
All this white stuff's hard to take.

Spring won't come, can't find an oriole.
That's why rap is my editorial.
I won't do news, I won't be political.
If there's a movie or a play, I won't be
critical.
Won't talk religion, won't be pulpitical.

Traffic stops, don't need cops;
No one roams, stay-at-homes.
Watch the scene, all serene;
See it fall, snow is all.

Winter's flag is all unfurled.
God's in his heaven, all's white with the
world.

We should restructure education. It's the only
time we've got the little bastards under our
control

Chopin's prelude in E minor is immediately
recognized from its theme but the dynamics
stop the daydream It's not a piano anymore.
It's a million hands playing your life

somehow the tissues crave an occasional bath
in salt water; possibly a throwback to our
ancient ancestry

Bad luck is when God really pays attention to
how you're living your life.

NO QUESTIONS ASKED

none taken
say we've basked

in pools of Jamaican
willingly unmasked

LISTS

I have taken your name off, alours!
And now, PLEASE! I off yours !

ABSURDITIES

blurred ditties
like oddities
numbered odd titties
for word universities

psychoanalysis itself is a dirty game: two
people swapping the decomposing humors of the
human spirit yet observing the death of the
human elixir

YOU'RE A NEUROTIC IF

you are reading this
you think life and freedom are the same
thing
you would just as soon have a drink with your
therapist and forget the entire experience
you understand that the sound of a clock
ticking off every second of the time has
nothing to do with you
you would rather have the right to remain
talkative
you can't believe how long this list is going
to be
you have already read this once before
you haven't married your mistress
you have no shame especially in what you fail
to do with makeup.
you made the wrong choice between
estrangement and abuse
you realize you are now taking a test to
indicate how nuts you are
you treat pets as trapped dictators
you will remember next time that having a
son/attorney can work both ways in court
you r promise to the internet turned to
slavery
you are the only last-chair violinist with a
knife in his back
you are perfectly comfortable that this is
all about you
you r victims seem happier than do the
victims of others
you treat a warning like any other dare
you r letters to the editor are always
printed with the good parts edited out

you r wife has become an auctioneer brought
into your life to do appraisals
You once said at a party that the Easter
bunny is the one animal that knows how to
give eggs without f***ing first
you think Passover comes from the word
"Turnpike"
you smile in pleasure at your self-portrait
in a mirror but it's way past closing time
you thought you die and go to hell, not the
other way around
you kept your money after the divorce and
lost yourself
you have a watch that is not right twice a
day
you are always two drinks away from romance
you should be at least a little concerned
that the rainbows are chasing you
you promised the taxi driver you'd tip better
the next time
you have a tragic daring that usually springs
up after midnight
you and I disagree on just about everything;
well, wait a minute, you disagree on that
you re afraid you have to read these all over
again

THE LORD'S PRIOR

Now please, God, don't give me any pain to
draw me away from You.

"Thank you, God!" is
all I know.

No rhyme became of this
.......a l t h o u g h........

I once went with my father when he played the piano in a silent movie theater.

and the audience took a gasp...

He would come home from his job in a comical mood

He sat me down at the keyboard

THAT'S ALL IT TOOK

Who Decided

You have to close your eyes when you sneeze.

You have to hold your breath if it's a long kiss

You have to embrace yourself in a sudden breeze.

You have to jog as a mile's as good as a miss.

Slight of Hand

When the trumpets end their summoning laugh.

And a lovely lady Is sawn in half.

Never since this trick began, such separation tried on man.

Prayerplayer

The Piano man
had them

Down on
their knees

When the chauffeur
came in, told him,

"Please find
your keys."

The Tounge Dynasty

The tongue hates rest

But silent tongue's best

Good with spinach, too

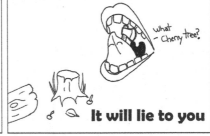

It will lie to you

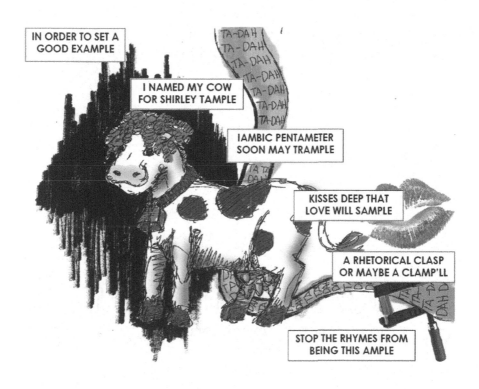

SO THE POINT WAS...

"TIC TOCK TOW" IS THE LAST THING THE FALLING CLOCK SAID AS IT FELL.

retromingent

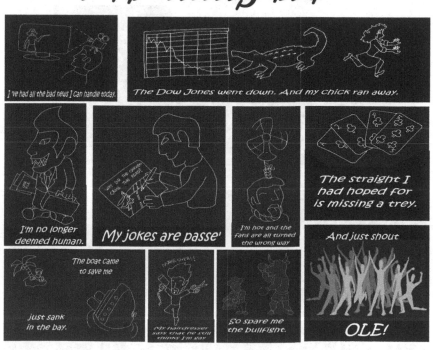

The Aegis of Man

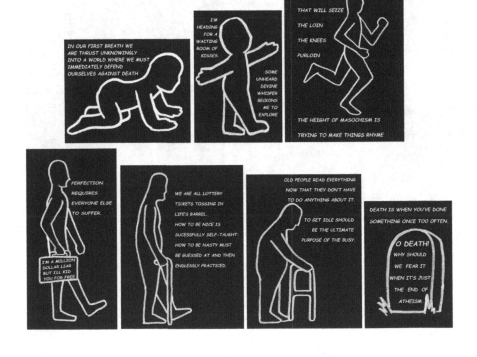

IN OUR FIRST BREATH WE
ARE THRUST UNKNOWINGLY
INTO A WORLD WHERE WE MUST
IMMEDIATELY DEFEND
OURSELVES AGAINST DEATH

I'M
HEADING
FOR A
WAITING
ROOM OF
KISSES.

SOME
UNHEARD
DEVINE
WHISPER
BECKONS
ME TO
EXPLORE

LOVE'S A DISEASE

THAT WILL SEIZE

THE LOIN

THE KNEES

PURLOIN

THE HEIGHT OF MASOCHISM IS

TRYING TO MAKE THINGS RHYME

PERFECTION
REQUIRES
EVERYONE ELSE
TO SUFFER.

I'M A MILLION
DOLLAR LIAR
BUT I'LL KID
YOU FOR FREE

WE ARE ALL LOTTERY
TICKETS TOSSING IN
LIFE'S BARREL.
HOW TO BE NICE IS
SUCESSFULLY SELF-TAUGHT:
HOW TO BE NASTY MUST
BE GUESSED AT AND THEN
ENDLESSLY PRACTICED.

OLD PEOPLE READ EVERYTHING
NOW THAT THEY DON'T HAVE
TO DO ANYTHING ABOUT IT.

TO GET IDLE SHOULD
BE THE ULTIMATE
PURPOSE OF THE BUSY.

DEATH IS WHEN YOU'VE DONE
SOMETHING ONCE TOO OFTEN.

O DEATH!
WHY SHOULD
WE FEAR IT
WHEN IT'S JUST
THE END OF
ATHEISM.